HERE
BE
MONSTERS

Being
An Anthology
Of
Gothic Monstrosities
In
Heavy Meter
And
Rhyme

By
The Reverend Doctor

Matt Lake

Baron of Sealand,
Resident of the United States of America

In Which Country This Volume was Printed
In This Year of the Common Era

QUARTO PRIMUS MMXV
QUARTO SECUNDUS MMXX

Here Be Monsters

by

The Reverend Doctor Matt Lake,
Baron of the Island Nation of Sealand

This and other b ooks by Matt Lake may be purchased by contacting the publisher and author at www.questionable.info

Published by Questionable.Info (established 2001) in the dot-info domain space of the World Wide Web of Cyberspace, and Media, Pennsylvania.

Printed in the United States of America

FROM

A

DICTIONARY

OF THE

ENGLISH LANGUAGE:

By SAMUEL JOHNSON, A. M.

Ho'RROUR. *n f.* [*horror*, Latin; *horreur*, French.]
Terrour mixed with deteftation; a paffion compounded
fear and hate, both ftrong.

HU'MOUR. *n. f.* [*humeur*, French; *humor*, Latin.]
Grotefque imagery; jocularity; merriment.

LONDON,
Printed by W. STRAHAN,
For J. and P. KNAPTON; T. and T. LONGMAN; C. HITCH and L. HAWES;
A. MILLAR; and R. and J. DODSLEY.
MDCCLV.

DEATH BECOMES A LIMERICK

OR

TO INCREASE ITS INTELLECTUAL APPEAL
A HAIKU
IN THE IRISH FORMAT

Knock knock," came a voice with no face.
"Who's there?" I enquired into space
"DEATH!" he replied.
"Death wh- ?" Then I died,
Thinking, "Damn! But that joke's in poor taste."

THE MOST DEGRADING IDEA
IN THE HISTORY OF
HUMAN THOUGHT

BEING A SONNET
IN
SHAKESPEAREAN FORMAT

I have a thought so vile I cannot speak it.
I'd be ashamed to hear the words aloud.
If my friends could hear it, they would freak—it
's the kind of thought that should be disavowed.

This thought, so harsh it owns me like a curse,
Spoils every interaction, every day.
It taints my world; my days grow worse and worse.
Yet it keeps me living, in its own strange way.

I'll take it to my deathbed; then I'll speak.
This thought shall pass from synapses to air
And leave my body emptied, happy, weak;
Relieved of that idea it had to bear.

"Come close, children. This secret must be heard.
And once you hear it, don't repeat a word."[i]

---

[i] *If, and only if, you feel you are strong enough to carry the burden of the most degrading thought in the history of human thought, turn the page.*

FOR YOUR NOTES

WE HAVE MET BEFORE

AND YOU BLOCKED IT OUT OF YOUR MIND
IN AN AUTONOMIC REACTION
SPURRED BY A SENSE OF
SELF-PRESERVATION

I'm the saboteur who slipped the fly into your ointment.
I was the man on the grassy knoll.
I'm the engineer of your every disappointment.
I'm the chunk of grit inside your breakfast roll.

Every time you slip up on the steps to your apartment,
I'm the one who placed that patch of black ice for your shoe.
When your promotion went to that young dunce in your
department,
I'm the one who shredded all the paperwork from you.

Every time you lose your purse, your keys, or peace of mind,
Look no further for a culprit: I'm the one you'll find.

I was the serpent in the Garden of Eden.
In the Land of Oz, you've seen my flying monkeys, and my
broom.
I helped out the Nazis during World War Two in Sweden.
You'll never see the Antichrist and me in the same room.

Every time your miss your bus on a wet and dismal day
It was me who set the clock behind a bit on your smartphone
And then I hacked your weather app, so that on your way

You thought it would be fine to leave your umbrella at home.

I do research all day long and lie awake at night to scheme
Of yet more ways of making your life seem like a bad dream.

Please allow me to introduce myself
I'm a man of cruel taste and big fortune
I'm the man who sold the world the Elf on the Shelf
And a dozen ways per day to importune:

1. I designed the DMV
2. The IRS's Schedule C
3. Everything you've bought that breaks
   one day past warranty
4. The all-pervasive presence of political punditry
5. At least a dozen channels of reality TV
6. The honking of a car horn for no reason you can see
7. Ill-fitting lids on take-out cups that make spill your
   tea
8. Infomercials urging you to be all you can be
9. Calling flies in Chardonnay a kind of irony
10. Meaning *metaphorically* but saying *literally.*
11. Billy Ray Cyrus (and Miley)
12. Star Wars (Episodes I through III)

Who's behind all that? It's me!

Every time you feel like balling up an angry fist
Direct your punch at me 'cause it's the reason I exist.

A SMALL SELECTION OF IRISH HAIKU

NOT SPONSORED
BY THE
JAPANESE MINISTRY OF TOURISM

Here's a tape that I'd like you to view,
Full of static and weirdness, it's true.
There's a girl in a well
Who will send you to Hell
'Cause the name on the tape is Ringu[i].

☺ ☺ ☺

Kuchi-sake Onna[ii] made me shriek
When I stopped in Japan just last week.
"Am I pretty?" she said
"Say 'no' and you're dead!
Say 'yes' and I'll slice up your cheek."

---

i This 1998 horror movie, directed by Hideo Nakata, was remade in English in 2002 by
director Gore Verbinski. The U.S. movie title is a direct translation of the original Japanese
title: *The Ring*.

ii This malicious ghost appears before victims carrying scissors and wearing a surgical mask
that conceals her deformity—a mouth that is slit at the corners. She challenges her victims
with a question about her beauty. The only possible outcomes for the people Kuchi -sake
Onna challenges are death or mutilation.

I'M MARRIED
TO A MEMBER OF THE LIVING DEAD

My house is the horror of the neighborhood.
No-one comes around here, and nobody should.
Children flee in terror when my missus appears.
Security forces can't allay their fears.
Our presence on the sidewalk fills pedestrians with dread,
'Cause I'm married to a member of the Living Dead.

It started out quite simply, as complex things can do,
I saw her by the pale moonlight—her lips were pale blue—
Her cold dead hands were clenched so tight,
But still I pried the gun from them, that cold and dreadful
night.
I could have dragged her to the crematorium, but, instead,
I married that member of the Living Dead.

The wedding service was a sight to see:
Held in a chapel in a cemetery.
She gave me her hand and I took it with a smile
And dropped it in my pocket as I walked down the aisle.
With a grin on my face and confetti on my head
I was proud to be the bridegroom of the Living Dead.

The reception? A collection of family and ghouls
We all got on together, like drunken fools.
They ran out of food, which could have spoilt the fun
But they called for paramedics on 9-1-1.
When they were eaten up, they called for cops instead.
It was a heck of a night of the Living Dead.

As we walked out together, stump in hand,
I suspected that the living wouldn't understand.
Those busybody neighbors began to make a fuss
"She's a reanimated zombie, not like us!"
Of course, they're in no danger: They've got nothing to fear,
Because it's brains that she likes eating—and there's none of
them 'round here.

"But why does she like him? And what's he see in her?"
I hear the questions ringing, and only answer's "Sir!
I've got a lot of brains and she wants them for her lunch,
And I keep a helmet on 'cause I have a kind of hunch
That she'll keep on coming back if my brains are wrapped in
lead
And I long for each Return of the Living Dead."

My reanimated missus, from her head down to her feet,
Is as colorful a character as you could hope to meet:
Her eyes are red; her skin is grey; her tongue's a pallid green;
And she knows her H.P. Lovecraft, if you know what I
mean!
She's got more brains between her teeth than you have in
your head,
And that is why I'm married to my bride, who's Living
Dead.

ANOTHER IRISH HAIKU

NOT SPONSORED BY THE MINISTRY OF TOURISM
FOR THE
NORTHERN REACHES OF THE UNITED KINGDOM,
OR
WHY NOT VISIT THE SCOTTISH LOWLANDS THIS
SUMMER?

The clan of the vile Sawney Beane [i]
Were worse than the worst Halloween[ii]
They were so steeped in sin
They slept with their kin
And ate humans for dinner! Obscene!

---

[i] Alexander "Sawney" Beane was a legendary Scottish villain whose family terrorized the coast around Ballantrae in the 1400s. Their crimes are covered in quite enough detail in the poem.

[ii] The general consensus is that the worst Halloween is a toss-up between *Halloween Resurrection* (2002) or *Halloween III: Season of the Witch* (1982).

RAVEN II

A RETURN TO NIGHT'S PLUTONIAN SHORE
OR
THE SEQUELS OF
EDGAR ALLAN POE

Twice upon a midnight dreary
While I pondered o'er the query
"Is there yet balm in Gilead?"
Suddenly there came a sound
Muffled, like cotton wrapped around
A watch, a tell-tale beating sound
That made men think me mad.

For I had penned verse with no equal
And tales that clamor'd for a sequel
And so the public called for more!
More noises at my window lattice;
More pondering where that damned black cat is;
More dark despair that men adore.
More men walled up in drunken revels
More black-feathered bird-shaped devils
This time saying "Furthermore..."

So the sequels came a-thumping
Thumping at my chamber door
The first one that the public's craving
Is, of course, *Son of the Raven*
With a prequel called "I Found Lenore."
And after these, a brand new scene:
As walls collapse with a mighty crack,
As *Fortunato Striketh Back*
And before too long...*The Tell-Tale Spleen* .

A victim is found with his belly slit
In *The Pendulum in Another Pit*.

Then a crazy scholar, diseased in the brain,
Brings his cousin a little peace
In *Dental Implants for Berenice*
And notching up some further pain
A tale to take away your breath:
A Second Masque…for the Yellow Death!
And *Usher's House, Rebuilt Again.*

ENOUGH!
        These horrors are no more
Erased by the raven at my chamber door
Whom I obey as he starts to implore
"Don't do sequels! Never bore!"
And so I won't. Forevermore!

AN IRISH HAIKU
TO HONOR THE MEMORIES OF
TWO MERCHANTS OF MENACE,
THE DEARLY DEPARTED WRITER RICHARD MATHESON
AND ACTOR, ART COLLECTOR, AND MAN ABOUT TOWN
VINCENT PRICE
OR
BEFORE HE BUILT EDWARD SCISSORHANDS,
HE SAVED HUMANITY

The Last Man on Earth, Vincent Price
Had his story re-edited, twice:
As The Omega Man,
I Am Legend (I Am),
Though a Hammer Film
          would have been nice

CHRISTMAS NIGHT OF THE LIVING DEAD

BEING A CELEBRATION OF LIFE
AND AFTERLIFE
AND MYSTERIOUS MEAT FOODSTUFFS
IN A SEASON OF GOODWILL
TOWARD MEN AND ZOMBIES

CHRISTMAS NIGHT OF THE LIVING DEAD

The undead in Monroeville liked Christmas a lot
With the Mall full of shoppers, well, how could they not?
There were big ones and small ones, all juicy and sweet
Those fleshy ripe shoppers were ready to eat.

But the zombies had eaten before they set out
And the food slowed them down as they shuffled about
It took them so long to arrive at the town
That the stores were all closed and the mall was locked
down.
Could they snack on a shopper right now? They could not.
So they stood there, confused, in the car parking lot.
Yes!
They stood there confused and they sniffed at the air
In hopes that Saint Nicholas soon would be there
For he was the juiciest fleshpot of all
And the zombies awaited him outside the mall

Now winter's a time when we all like to feast
From humans to zombies to every wild beast
So when the mall closed, all the shoppers went down
To a big winter party just outside of town.
For we all love our food when the weather gets cold,
And the food at this feast was a sight to behold!

Some wanted clementines, cake, and mixed nuts
Or canes made of candy, no ifs, ands, or buts!
Hot chocolate to warm them on nights bathed in snow
And the Scottish food haggis (It's best not to know
What they put in that stuff—let's keep it a mystery—
But hey, it's kept Scottish folk warm throughout history)

The Germans brought sausages stuffed with...surprise

The English brought kidneys and steak in their pies
For dessert, there were dishes with lightly spiced apple
And a great Pennsylvania dish, known as fried scrapple
That's meaty and spicy, made of...well...who knows what?
But on cold days, I'll tell you, it's certainly hot.

But they weren't serving scrapple out there at the Mall
They were serving it at the Community Hall
So the zombies were lacking the holiday cheer
Because Santa, they feared, would not ever appear.

Then the scrapple-smell wafted clear down to the mall
And with it, the whiff of a man known to all
The aroma of pine trees, and cookies, and milk
And a red suit worn over a shirt of fine silk
A jolly old elf-smell, with fur and a beard

And one of the zombies groaned "Guys! This is weird...
That mystery-meat smell is wafting so thick,
But under it all, I can smell good Saint Nick!"
Yes, the zombies could smell him, out there in the street
And they stumbled towards him, in search of fresh meat.

As the folk of Monroeville sat down at the feast
They had no idea that, off to the east,
Was a shambling army of man-eating fiends,
So they partied as if it was still Halloween.
And the visions that danced in their party-time heads
Were of brisket and latkes and plates of warm breads
Of pierogies and stollen cake, foods of that ilk
And pudding and fruitcake and mugs of warm milk
Of Stilton and crackers and tea brewed quite strong
And afterwards, plenty of music and song
In short, as the zombies approached for *their* food
Monroeville was steeped in a partying mood

Except for a smart little girl in the hall
Who kept asking questions of one and of all
This clever young lass was young Jennifer-Sue
Who was smart 'cause she knew just how little she knew
(If you look at a thing and want knowledge to grow
You find somebody smart in the room that you know
And you ask them to tell you, if they'd be so kind,
And that is the way that you fill up your mind.)

"What's in that scrapple and haggis?" she'd say
But her father and mother just shooed her away
And the chef in the kitchen would likewise not talk
And the mayor and the minister just took a walk
So Jennifer-Sue made a note in her book
To go to the library one day for a look
Because she had knowledge that most people lack:
You can learn many things from a good almanac.

Then Jennifer-Sue looked around and about
And saw some bright statues and gave out a shout
"That's Jesus, I think, lying there in the straw!
Is that the same Jesus who's nailed to the wall?
That kid and the guy with the cross and the beard;
Are they the same person? Now isn't that weird?"

And the folks of Monroeville let out a loud shout
And laughed at what Jennifer-Sue spoke about
It wasn't a cruel laugh, but one of good cheer.
Though soon, it gave way to a scream of real fear
For the door to the hall burst apart with a clatter
And the folk looked around to see what was the matter
And what to their wondering eyes should appear
But a slobbering zombie a-stumbling near

Then the men of Monroeville went on the attack
And they pushed back that ghoul; closed the door to a crack,

When the rest of the zombies began to arrive
And burst through that door...would the humans survive?

They grabbed a big table and pushed it, legs first,
At the horde, hoping they'd be completely dispersed
But the zombies pushed back, and they groaned in their pain
Because all they could think about was Santa's brain!
The smell of that fleshpot engendered such hunger
Like the warm smell of scrapple had, when they were
younger.

So the zombies pushed one way, the humans, the other
As their eyes met, hearts melted, as brother faced brother
For some of the zombies were family and friends
And it's hard to view loved ones through that kind of lens.

The two sides were well matched; neither side budged
But at this rate, the humans would lose, as they judged:
Because zombies don't tire; they just keep on going
And the humans could feel just how tired they were growing.

"Let's throw something at them!" The pushing men shouted
And the crowd grabbed for things that might help—but I
doubt it—
For the knives, forks, and plates that they grabbed, aimed,
and tossed
In an effort that, frankly, was doomed to be lost
Because though tossing tableware seems rather drastic
They weren't good projectiles; but made out of plastic

Then a voice rose above all the groans and the shouting
"We can get through this, people, we shouldn't be doubting
For we know what this season is really about
It's all about faith; not at all about doubt!
And that boy in the straw in the crib—there! By you!—
He rose from the dead, and the zombies did too!

And although they are tireless, hungry, and strong
I'm sure there's a way we can all get along!"

It was Jennifer-Sue. But the grown-ups said "Fie!
You're a kid, you don't get it! We're all going to die!
They don't care that it's Christmas, and all of that stuff
These zombies will kill us--enough is enough!
Let's all give up now, at least we'll die quickly!"

But Jennifer-Sue wouldn't quit, and she slickly
Picked up some scrapple, and sausages too
And a slice of fried haggis, which she then threw
At the zombie horde being restrained by the table
She threw just as skillfully as she was able:
Those mystery-meat pieces shot out through the air
And into the mouths of the zombies right there.

And the story they tell of what happened that day
Is: The zombies stopped pushing, and started to say,
"This tastes better than brains...I ate this as a boy
And it makes me remember that Christmassy joy
I could eat more of this, for my old mother's sake
And chow down on some slices of that stollen cake!"

And the folks of Monroeville say *that* was the time
That the zombies spoke English--and spoke it in rhyme!

Zombies took that long table the humans were shovin'
And set it down gently, and went to the oven
And brought out some more of that piping hot scrapple
To serve to the humans, with pies full of apple
Then they served themselves up a heaping great plateful
And the humans could tell they were ever so grateful.

So the humans and zombies sat down to the feast

Oh, they partied like neighbors—that's saying the least!
The zombies swore they would henceforth cause no trouble
The humans said that, for their part, that goes double!

And from that day forth, through Monroeville, they said,
"At Christmas, we welcome the formerly dead
The people who rose from the grave are invited
To eat with the humans, who would be delighted
To share all their haggis, and scrapple, and stuff
Till the zombies and humans have eaten enough."

So after your party, one Christmassy night
When you've eaten with friends, and you're feeling alright
Take some time to be quiet and listen quite closely
For according to legend, you'll often hear, mostly,
The voice of a girl wafting through the night air
As she asks one more question to folks gathered there.
It's Jennifer-Sue, and you'll hear her say
"Just what do they put in this stuff anyway?"

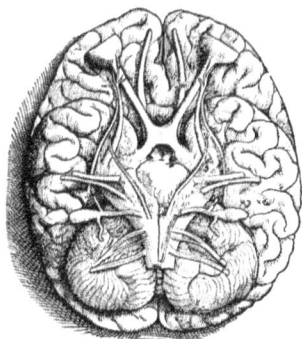

A SELECTION OF IRISH HAIKU

CELEBRATING THE VAMPIRE
OR
THREE PAINS IN THE NECK

It's a truth universally known
That the vampire's victims will groan
At Dracula's bite,
For the fangs that affright
Are not fibrous dysplasia of bone.

🦇 🦇 🦇

Horror fans just can't agree
On who the best vampire might be
Not Twilight's young cast
But a blast from the past
Like Lugosi or Christopher Lee.

🦇 🦇 🦇

As I looked in the mirror, I saw
No reflection: It filled me with awe.
But a pain in my neck
Made me cry out "Oh heck!
That's the last time I hug Draculaw!"

🦇 🦇 🦇

AN IRISH HAIKU
CELEBRATING THE NEW ENGLAND
MASTER OF MENACE
CREATOR OF HUGE FORMLESS SLOBBERING THINGS THAT
GROPINGLY SQUEEZE THEIR GELATINOUS GREEN IMMENSITY
INTO THE TAINTED OUTSIDE AIR IN THE POISON CITY OF
MADNESS, H.P. LOVECRAFT

In R'lyeh old Cthulhu abides
With slimy green rocks on all sides
Cyclopean styles
Stretch for miles and miles
Through your dreams the Old Great One strides.

THE MYTH OF CONCEPTION

BEING A POEM ABOUT
HUMAN REPRODUCTIVE BEHAVIOUR
AND THE AFTERMATH
THEREOF,
IN TERMS BEST NOT SHOWN
TO THOSE OF A DELICATE SENSIBILITY,
BY WHICH WE MEAN
THOSE CREATURES MALE AND FEMALE
(BUT MOSTLY MALE)
OF SUCH FRAGILE CONFIDENCE
THAT THE NOTION OF SHARING CREDIT
IS ANATHEMA

We are the result of a hero's quest
The biology books seem to tell us
The product of one single conqueror sperm
Leaving millions of also-rans jealous
An alpha-male gamete that outran the rest
Stormed the castle, and brought things to term.

It's a well-crafted hero myth—still, it's a myth
And the actual story's more strange:
Gametes that collaborate get to be born
(Versed in the language of protein exchange);
Swap ions to activate each other with,
Sharing all things in order to spawn.

It was working together that made me and you—
Well, that, and a few trillion bacteria too.

KRAMPUS ON THE SHELF

BEING A TRADITION AS OLD
AS SANTA HIMSELF
AND CONSIDERABLY
OLDER
THAN
FROSTY
AND
RUDOLPH
AND
BUDDY THE ELF

KRAMPUS ON THE SHELF

Halloween's over. Thanksgiving has passed.
The trees and the lights have appeared at last.
In the stores, all the Christmas stuff's out on the shelves
The tinsel, the snowglobes, the lights, and the elves—

And right about now, it can hardly be missed,
The grown-ups start talking about Santa's list!
"Are you naughty or nice?" they all want to know
And each time that they ask you, anxieties grow.

You try to be nice—or at least, well, you should—
But what do they mean? Because no-one's ALL good!
We all get annoyed and do things we regret—
Even grown-ups—and yet we forgive and forget.

So what about Santa's list—naughty or nice?
Well, I'll tell you, but listen, I won't tell you twice.
This secret has been kept for many a year
Santa just keeps the Nice list—there's no need to fear!

If you're basically good, you will get your reward
If you're rotten right through, then prepare for my horde
For I keep the list of the Naughty, I swear
Yes! I am the Krampus! You'd better beware!

I assemble my list from close observation
I spy and I phone-tap with great dedication
You may see me or hear me as I skulk about
And know this about me: I'm no friendly scout

You'd better believe that I'm not very nice
I'm making a list and I'm checking it twice
And if you are on it, you'd better beware!
I'll punish you hard, and I won't even care!

So how will you know that you're there on my list?
I'll show you some clues that you'll find hard to miss!
Look around till you see me—up high on the shelf
And check out my hands to see for yourself!

Am I holding a chain to be used for restraint?
Do you think that that's good? 'Cause it certainly ain't!
I chain up the mean kids and laugh as they weep,
And scare most of them straight as their parents all sleep!

Am I holding some birch sticks? Well that's even worse!
If I'm holding up birch sticks then somebody's cursed!
Those sticks will thrash kids who are thoroughly rotten.
If you see them, you'll know that I haven't forgotten!

So there are your warnings—the chain and the sticks.
If you see them, you'd better give up your mean tricks
'Cause a beating's by far not the worst I can do
Say your prayers, cause you don't want this happening to
you:

If you look round your house on one cold winter day
And I'm up on your shelf or your couch or duvet
Look around or behind me, in front and in back
And see if I've brought my big Krampussy sack

If I have, you're in danger because you've been awful
And punishment's coming, that's cruel but it's lawful
You'll be stuffed in that sack—it's so sad to tell—
And I'll carry you off in it, straight down to...

Well...

I think you're now wise to my place in the world
I'm the Krampus and I know every boy and each girl
Most of you, Santa will shower with love
The rest of you suffer the Krampus's shove

So every year on St. Nicholas Night
I'll come to your home, not to give you a fright
But remind you that I keep the naughty kids' list
And no one who's on it will ever be missed
They'll be gone and I think that is all for the best
For peace upon earth, and goodwill to the rest.

THE KITCHEN WITCH OF CHRISTMAS

BEING A TALE OF THE
MOST FAMOUS WOMAN IN ITALY
LA BEFANA

Two weeks after Christmas, the house was all quiet
But so messy it looked like the scene of a riot
There were presents all strewn from the rug to the walls
With tinsel and holly all decked in the halls
You could tell we'd had Christmas, and New Year's as well
Oh the parties we'd had! Oh the tales we could tell!
But now we were resting all snug in our beds
With the hint of an ache and a cold in our heads
On that January night as we dozed in our cots
There arose a great clatter—Did it scare us? Yes, lots!
A crash and a thud and a cough and a thump
And a voice that exclaimed, "Will you look at this dump!
This can't be the place...Those kings must be wrong
Or perhaps I'm just lost...But I've been lost so long!"
I turned to Mamma who just waved to the phone
And said "Call the police! They've invaded our home!"
But I knew in my heart we had nothing to dread
So I smiled and I winked and I jumped out of bed
And what did I see as I walked down the stair
But a strange-looking woman with long wild hair
She stood in the kitchen—I could see her quite clearly—
With a long witch's broom that she held onto dearly
She swept up the soot as it happened to fall
And she swept it so well that she tidied it all.
It was so strange to see her I gave out a cry
And she twisted around, a strange look in her eye.

"Are you the child?" she said "Are you the One
That the kings talked about? That I've looked for so long?"
She could see that I wasn't, but she wasn't too sad
She just smiled and reached for a basket she had
"I brought him some gifts, but I've not found him yet
So I'll give one to you. Come and see what you'll get"
As she looked in her basket who should enter the room
But Mamma in her kerchief—she looked at the broom
And the soot and the basket and let out a roar!
"Do you know who this is? Who has swept up our floor?
She's Befana! My grandma from Italy said
She's the witch of the kitchen, a shawl on her head,
Who looks for a baby from long, long ago
Like the three old wise men from the Bible, you know.
She's been lost all this time but she comes into homes
And leaves gifts for the children and then…off she roams."
"But it's long after Christmas," said I — "Not tonight!
It's the Twelfth Night of Christmas" Of course! She was
right
"On the twelfth night of Christmas, this January night,
La Befana will visit—Or at least, she just might"
The old witch looked up and she gave me a fig
It's weird kind of gift. It's not very big.
Then she looked at Mamma with an odd kind of grin
And gave her some coal and said "Go on! Tuck in!"
Well, I chewed on my fig and it didn't taste bad
But Mamma only stood with her coal, looking sad
La Befana reached down and she grabbed her own lump
And started to eat it "It's candy, you chump!"

She crunched it a while and stuck her tongue out

And Mamma was so shocked, that she let out a shout
Her tongue had turned black from the rock-candy coal
But Befana just laughed like a merry old soul
Then she grabbed up her basket and jumped on her broom
And she waved and she flew quickly out of the room
She flew up to the sky
Where the airplanes all go
And her voice rang out clear
To the valley below
And I heard her call out
As she zoomed out of sight:
"Merry Christmas to all—and
To all…a Twelfth Night."

A SMALL SELECTION
OF IRISH HAIKU

CELEBRATING THE MONOCHROME FILM TRADITION
AND THREE
OF ITS
CELEBRATED MONSTERS
(ONE OF WHICH IS HUMAN)

If there's one thing more creepy than brains
It's movies that go to great pains
To cover the head
Of the villain instead
(See: Invisible Man, with Claude Rains).

❋ ❋ ❋

I nervously watched the full moon
If the Wolf Man attacked, I would swoon
But I stood on the shore
And was worried far more
By what lived in the deep Black Lagoon.

THE SUNTANNED VAMPYR

When the sun comes up and the moon fades out
I rise and howl, I start to twist and pout
I jump in a Miata that I call The Beast
'Cause I'm a suntanned vampyre looking for a feast
I'm thin
Full of sin
I'm lord of the undead, full of melanin

I drive to the beach with the ragtop down
Then I change into my spandex speedos and gown
I check out all the food so skimpily dressed
Suck yoghurt from the veins of the doubly blessed
I'm male
Not so pale
I live in Santa Barbara
A Hungarian folk tale

Well I trawl California on a vampyre quest
Sinking my fangs into the very best
And my favorite meal is vegetarian
'Cause their blood's got less cholesterol, more riboflavin
Undead
Lips red
And two sharp fangs sprouting in my head

I'm the buffest neck-sucker that you ever saw
I want your jugular, baby, right between my jaws
Give it to me, baby, you won't regret

'Cause I've got a new sensation that you haven't felt yet
I suck
And you're in luck
'Cause you're going to live forever from my nip. And tuck.

A VISIT FROM THE BELZNICKEL

BEING A GERMANIC GIFT-GIVING DISCIPLINARIAN
WHO MAKES SANTA LOOK LIKE
A RIGHT JOLLY OLD ELF
OR
AN ANTIDOTE TO *THE NIGHT BEFORE CHRISTMAS*

A VISIT FROM THE BELZNICKEL

On a night in December I'll never forget,
The best family party we'd ever had yet
Was just wrapping up; we'd exchanged all our gifts,
And the snow, it had started to come down in drifts.

My father was cheerful; my uncles were loud
And we all of us started to sing as a crowd.
Christmas was coming, 'twas practically here
And we all celebrated another great year.

It could have been perfect, it would have been too,
Except for the presence of my cousin Drew
Now Drew's not so bad, just a bit of a brat,
And this near to Christmas, I'll leave it at that.

And then, just as Grandpa was starting to snore
Somebody brought out the Clement C. Moore
"Not *The Night Before Christmas!*" my cousin complained
But he need not have worried or acted so pained,

For just as my uncle cracked open the tome
A terrible clatter rang out through our home.
The window panes rattled as if whacked with a stick
And I knew in an instant it wasn't Saint Nick.

"The Belznickel!" Grandpa cried out to my Dad
"The Belznickel's come here to punish the bad!
The wicked young children who haven't done right
The Belznickel takes them away in the night!

"He wraps them in chains and he drags them away
And he brandishes birch whips, or that's what they say
He carries a barrel, they say, full of treats
To trick the young children, whom he wants to beat.

But I thought he was gone now," he shivered with cold,
"I thought he'd been left back in Europe of old
In the deep old dark woods where the wolves used to howl
With his birch whip and chains and the horns on his cowl.

But that rattling of windows, that birch whip I see
It's the Belznickel, kids, and he's not come for me
He's come for the bad kids—are there any in here?—
If there are, let me tell you, you've something to fear!"

Then the doorway flew open and in it appeared
A man dressed in furs, 'twas the man I most feared
The cowl on his head sprouted horns on each side.
And all round his waist, a long chain was tied,

And tucked in his belt was a bundle of sticks
For whacking young children who played naughty tricks.
The Belznickel stared with a twist of his head
That gave us to know we had plenty to dread
He reached back to his barrel and narrowed his eyes,

And said "Hey there, children, I've got a surprise!
You've all been so good that I've brought you a treat"
And he rolled golden apples towards our cold feet.
I looked at my cousin and knew he had lied.

Drew hadn't been good; he'd not even tried
The Belznickel lied, and I saw at once why:
He was holding his whip, a cruel look in his eye
I motioned to Drew but he looked confused.

"He's holding a whip that he's hoping to use"
Drew caught on to my meaning, scared halfway to death
He moved not a muscle. He just held his breath.

And I told the Belznickel, "Why sir, you're so kind
But we don't deserve what you're leaving behind,
We can't take your presents, but just down the street
Our neighbors' young children would love such a treat.

They're much more deserving, and we've got enough
A wonderful meal and lots of neat stuff…"
My voice trailed off and I waited to see
Even more of the Belznickel's foul trickery.

But what to my wondering eyes did appear,
But the Belznickel smiling and spreading no fear.
His face, it had altered, the cruelty gone,
And he opened his mouth and thus he went on:

"So you've learned what Christmastide is all about
You don't clamor for more and more stuff, and don't shout
For things that you want but you don't really need
You understand Christmas is not about greed,

And because you're not greedy and show me respect
You'll escape with no beating; benign's my neglect"

And he turned on his heel, made his way through the door
And we knew that we would see him this winter no more.

But before he was gone, he turned back to say
"Don't ever be greedy around Christmas Day!
Next year, I will come down this road one more time
And I'll punish your greed, for I call it a crime!
But if you are not wicked, you need fear no fright.
Merry Christmas to all, and to all a good night!
And with that he was gone in the winter night's cold
And we had a gift that's more precious than gold
As we laughed once again with the season's good cheer
We'd escaped from the Belznickel's whip one more year!

A JAZZ-AGE SYNCOPATED
IRISH HAIKU

ON THE VEXED SUBJECT
OF LYCANTHROPY
AND ITS POSSIBLE CURE

The silver bullet tore my flesh and made me scream "Ow!"
It changed me in a vital way—I cannot say how
It might have been tragic
But the silver was magic
I used to be a werewolf, but I'm alright noooooOOOOooooow

THE SHADOWGHAST

BEING THE TALE OF
A CREATURE
NOT OF THIS WORLD
BUT VISIBLE
AT THE EDGES
OF OUR SIGHT

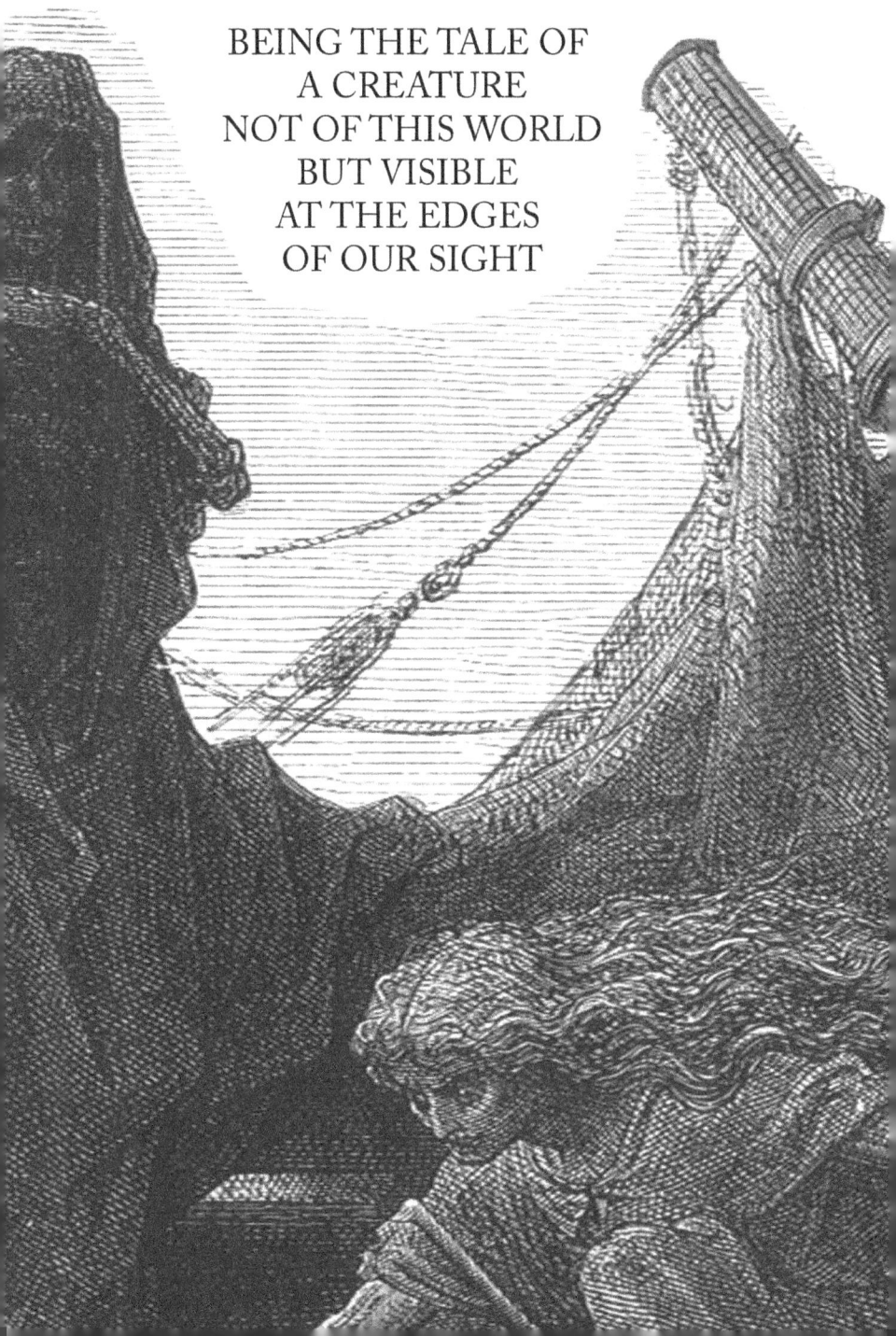

THE SHADOWGHAST

CANTO I
The Night of the Challenge

The wind was cold and at our backs;
We stood at midnight on the tracks
And stared into the tunnel, waiting for a sign.
I thought it was a stupid dare
That brought us standing, shivering there
I thought, "When it's all over, we'll be fine,"
We both ignored a chill at our spine,
"When it's all over we'll be fine."

They challenged us at the schoolyard gate
They called us afraid—that's a word we hate—
They said we lacked the courage to behave like men
They told us where to go when the sun went down—
To the trestle on the freight line, two miles out of town
Where the trains cross the river and the road, and then
Plunge into the tunnel running through the hill.
They said that brave boys go there, and it's quite a thrill

They said that men had died there, on the rails long ago
When the rains were so heavy that the ground began to flow
And dragged a mudslide in the path of a speeding train.
The men that died that day were mourned
And the railroad company, roundly warned
That the town could not endure another instance of such
pain.
So they engineered a sturdy tunnel through the hill

And the tunnel and its trestle both remain there still.

"Stand at midnight at the tunnel's mouth
Make sure that your right side is facing south
And stare through the tunnel till the clock strikes one.
Don't breathe a word and never blink
Don't pray or laugh, or even think.
Just stare through the tunnel till the ritual's done."
We assumed that this whole venture was all in fun
And that is how the creature won.

"Something will appear," they said as we walked by,
"You'll see him lurking in the corner of your eye,
And as soon as you see him, then all will be revealed.
For cowards, this secret is a mystery,
To the brave, like us, it's part of history."
So we accepted their challenge and our fate was sealed.
And so we stood there, wretchedly cold,
Hoping that our darkest fears would never unfold.

 The clock tower chimed in the middle of the night
As the twelfth chime echoed, the tunnel seemed so bright
But not from hidden magic; we were just used to the dark.
The staring and the cold made our eyeballs sting.
We stood and stared and waited for the final ring
Of the clock-tower, chiming one o'clock, when we could leave our mark,
Secure in the knowledge we had passed the test,
And possessed a hidden secret unknown to the rest.

We stood almost an hour before that man-made cave

The only sounds were wind, and the river's rippling wave
And the clattering of teeth in my companion's mouth.
The fear began to rise as minutes passed by
The shivering increased and we knew not why
The wind suddenly dropped, and in the distance from the
south
We heard the clock tower chiming one:
The sign that our ritual was finally done.

We blinked our eyes in silence and began to walk
Feeling far too idiotic to resort to talk
We felt those youths had played a prank on gullible young
boys
and so we walked in silence on the road to town.
Our eyes, still sore from staring, cast in sadness down.
Our footfalls and the stream, they were the only background
noise.
We walked along in silence deep
And longed to be at home, asleep.

CANTO II
The Break of Dawn

The morning sun sliced through a chink in the curtain—
A shaft of light and dust—and I could not be certain
That our night-time escapade had not been dreamed.
But I felt my heart lay heavy, there in my chest.
My limbs all ached; I yearned to have more rest,
Yet the time had to come to rise, and so it seemed
That our adventure had been real—and a real mistake—
And so, to chase off sleep, I gave my head a shake.

The shaft of light and dust from the curtain's crack
Shimmered slightly as I rose and yawned and stretched my
back
And cast a moving shadow across the wall.
"The limb of the old birch, shaken by a gust,
Casting leafy patterns on the wall...it must
Be that," my sleep-soaked mind surmised, and all
I could think of then was my morning chores:
The soap, the toothbrush, walk to school, and sundry other
bores.

I missed my friend on the walk to school. Not wanting to be
late
I walked alone up to the lurkers by the schoolyard gate
And could not resist the chance to raise a shout
"We stood at midnight on the track
We weren't afraid and never looked back
I guess that you don't know what it's all about."
The lurkers at the gate just smirked and said
"You'll see him soon enough, and you'll be dead."

"What do you mean by that?" I almost cried,
"A ghost appears to folks like you, and all who've seen it,
died."
Those lurkers at the schoolyard gate had done it one more
time
They taunted and they won, because we fell for it.
They measure you and judge, and they can tell you're fit
For mocking; so they perpetrate their crime
Make sure there are no witnesses, and then

Go on to find more victims, and taunt them over again.

It was then I thought I saw him, through the edges of my
sight,
My companion from the ritual on the tracks last night.
And I knew these taunts upset him more than me.
So I set out in his direction to lead him a different way
But as I turned to face my friend, well, what more can I say?
The image of him vanished—there was nothing left to see—
I turned back toward the school gate, and realized my fears:
The lurkers had another chance to pelt me with their jeers.

They day went by but my friend did not come
I missed him, of course, but my senses were numb
From too little sleep and too much aggravation.
So I resolved to visit him as soon as I could
Though I needed to rest, I knew that I should
Take that walk uphill from the station
Take a left turn and a right, and knock on his door
Give him homework, and leave, and nothing more.

But at his door, his mother waved me off, and turned away
"He's ill," she said, "Too ill." and that's all that she would
say,
Then shut the door in my expectant face.
She said the same the next day, and the next day still.
Her face was drawn with worry, and she herself looked ill
But every time I turned away, for a second, in that place
In the corner of my eye, I swear I saw him leaning
A little closer every time. And now I know the meaning.

CANTO III
The Shadow Falls

The wind was cold against my face
This evening. I increased my pace
Along the street that led to my friend's home.
I knew his folks would send me back again,
And claim he was still ill, and then
Demand I turn around and trudge back home alone.
But not tonight! I would not turn around.
No, not tonight. Tonight, I'd stand my ground.

The street was busy for that time of night
At almost every door a person stood, at the edge of my line
of sight
But I forged straight ahead to see my friend.
I reached his door, but instead of making sound
I quietly tried the handle, pushed it open, stood my ground.
The door swung open to a hallway; at the end
Of which a tall thin shadow faced
Me, dark and featureless, and my heart raced.

I flinched and blinked and gaped, and then
He wasn't there. My heart still pounded. I looked again,
And told myself I'd fallen into fear just like a child.
Those lurking taunters at the schoolyard gate
Had done their work; those people that I hate
Had planted fear inside my head; a fear that so beguiled
Me, it lodged an image inside me:
I was seeing things I could not see.

So I stepped across the threshold, crept along the hall,
Careful not to make a sound, I barely breathed at all
Until I reached the foot of the stair
When I heard voices, but could hear no word
A muttered conversation that could not be overheard
So of course, I paused and strained my ears there
But all I heard was "cannot see,"
A phrase that made no sense to me.

So step by silent step, I climbed the stairs
Crept past the reading nook with its cushioned chairs
And to the room in which my friend was lying
At the door I heard no sound
So I turned the handle, looked around
And opened up his door. His eyes were red from constant
crying
His face was pale, his mouth was strained
Into a caricature of a scream of pain.
"It's only me!" I hissed at him "I'm here!"
His eyes half-closed, which pushed out a tear
That slowly welled into a drop that slid across his face and
lost its form.
"He's here too," his gurgling voice sobbed out
"Can you see him too?" He cast his eyes about
As if his mind, unhinged, could see a swarm
Of hostile creatures all around.
He flinched at all these phantoms, cast his eyes down to the
ground.

He blinked. Then abject terror etched across his face
He thrashed his arms and legs all round the place

And gurgled from some place deep inside
His family's feet were hard upon the stairs
His mother's voice was chanting Catholic prayers
My back against the wall, I tried to hide
"Oh GOD!" he shouted, choked and finally sighed
"He's reaching out!" and muttered as he died.

CODA
Twilight in the Corner of my Eye

This place is cold. I don't know how I came
To be here, but I'm lying here just the same,
And looking all around me.
I dare not speak or even think
Or look away or even blink
I don't know how or why, but he has found me.
He is hiding in the shadows everywhere.
I cannot see him, but I know he's there.

SONG OF THE SIREN

BEING A LAMENTATION
OF THE IMPOSSIBLE LOVE
OF MAN FOR MERMAID

Strapped to the wheel, lashed to the mast, I hear
the song from out at sea; a keening
wistful teasing yearning sound, and she is near—
out there—perhaps drowning; the meaning
of her words, washed out by wind...it dips
beneath the storm-frothed waves. I crave the lips
that make that sound; I want them whispering
softly as they brush my ear; I cut my bonds
and leap--sink down, swim down , slithering
through clouds of plankton, jellyfish, and fronds
of kelp-my will to breathe is withering—
toward the song, toward a cave, and...stop.

Out she slides, smiling, saying "It's begun!
My eggs are in there. Call me when you're done."

A FOURTH FATE

The firstborn child of Darkness and the Night
—**Clotho**—span the thread from which all gloom
is made, extruding alphabets that might
Be used to make the words that seal our doom.

This wretched Fate's next siste r rolls out lives—
Or thread (it's hard to see this far away).
Lachesis measures out their length and strives
To be uncaring and unfair—the Greek gods' way.

The shears the next Fate wields determine how we die
Inevitable **Atropos,** who cannot turn
Decides the way we all will end—but won't say why—
All three avoid the blame for how their victims burn.

We need another Fate, an advocate exuding grace,
Who'll take our side, and punch her sisters in the face.

AN EPITAPH FOR OUR TIMES

I read an epitaph, or saw one in
a dream, and felt the need to read about
the life behind these words. It was foregone, in
case you wondered, that I would need to shout
this epitaph aloud before I could begin:

IF YOU LIVED HERE
YOU'D BE HOME ALREADY

It's a sentence I had read before, only
this time, it was carved in round and steady
letters upon a gravestone, stark and lonely.
Unlike the old Egyptians, whose tombs exalt
the great, and extol the vast achievements
of their kings, our tombs avoid the faults
of our deceased, and our bereavement.
We count a soundbite as a would-be win.

HORROR NOTES

BEING ADVICE FOR SURVIVING
SHOULD YOU SUDDENLY
FIND YOURSELF TRAPPED
IN A HORROR MOVIE

Just in case you've all forgotten,
zombies walking, damp and rotten,
mummies talking, wrapped in cotton,
teach us to go slack and swoon.

Rallying, we all break loose
Brandish torches, stakes, a noose,
And fishfood—which is just a ruse
For creatures from the Black Lagoon.

We load our guns with silver, then
We wait to hear a howling, when
A man turns wolf, as once again
He changes with the changing moon.

Take note, you fans of horror, do not cry!
And don't have sex or showers, or you'll die.

SIX SEXTILLION SLICK CICADAS
SLOWLY SHED THEIR SHELLS

STOP! The world's descendi ng into several types of hells.
The popping of the carcasses coats shoes with weird smells
The carnage carries choruses like loud funereal bells!
As six sextillion slick cicadas slowly shed their shells.

Erupting red-eyed creatures crawl from decades at their slumber
Coating trees and ground and walls and several kinds of lumber
And gorging all their predators, by virtue of their number
As six sextillion slick cicadas slowly shed their shells.

The noise that comes forth from these beasts will drive us a ll to drugs
Or off to CVS to search for sold-out ear plugs
You can't believe this racket comes from just a bunch of bugs
As six sextillion slick cicadas slowly shed their shells.

Seventeen years we've been at peace (unless you read the news)
This brood's been underground at several feet beneath our shoes
But they've emerged to give our eardrums a thorough bruise
As six sextillion slick cicadas slowly shed their shells.

These shiny sylph -winged mega-crickets coat the earth this year
They're eating them in Baltimore, washed down with local beer
And crunching carapace with car tires everywhere they steer
As six sextillion slick cicadas slowly shed their shells.

Let us be!
Set us free!
We can't endure the noise, you see!

Brood X wrecks our breakfast
Their sex calls grate our nerves to dust
Their awful screeching locust lust
Sends us psycho, as it must.

These six sextillion
Slick cicadas
Slowly shed their shells
(their inhibitions
                then their lives)
as, sick with sex,
They slide into silence,
Spawning-sated, incapacited

Set aside and now belated.

Sayonara, sap-suckers!
See you in seventeen summers.

PROLOGUE TO A TALE BY LOVECRAFT

Do not think me mad
(I'm not mad! I am not!)
But this is the truth that I live with:
I shall never sleep calmly again.

As the night slithers into my room
It is joined by a loathsome but nameless dread
A nameless gelatinous pulpy green slime
That comes seeping into my head.

This dark oozy thing —though a dream—is no dream
It is anything but ethereal
Its voice—not a voice—has a color.
It's black. With a darkness that's almost material.

Now hear the full tale of all that I've seen
And the nameless dread terrors I've heard.

The story begins with my uncle, who's dead
Who was jostled to death near the Bay
By a dark and mysterious nautical man
Who was quietly ushered away.

If only I'd known the things I know now
I would not have agreed to his will,
And read in his papers the things I would read,
The things that haunt me still

These things I must tell
So that none of you merge on this road with me, down into Hell,
And then join me in sinking to depths of despair.
Please don't join me.
I swear, I shall never sleep calmly again.

WHO IS THE ALBATWITCH?

The albatwitch is roaming 'round
In central Pennsylvania.
Who'd have thought this hallowed ground
Could actually sustain ya?

The small ape man this state adores
Lurks around in woods and bogs
Leaving trails of apple cores
Avoiding hikers and their dogs

Albatwitch, what are you? Are you ape or man?
Do you have a name we'd recognize, like Frank or Fred or Betty?
Let us know, please, if you can,
You half-sized, small-foot yeti.

FASTER FASTER SNALLYGASTER

Have you seen the Snallygaster?
On his wings he brings disaster
Flying fast and swooping faster
Faster! Faster! Snallygaster!

When the snallygaster flies
Like a dragon through the skies
Who knows what trouble he'll devise–
He's the snallygaster!
Tentacles squirm upon his head
Grab his victims, squeeze them dead
His gaping maw drips bloody red
He's the snallygaster!

Through fields of hairy golden aster
Teeth as white as alabaster
Comes that bringer of disaster
Faster! Faster! Snallygaster!

YOU KNOW WHO YOU ARE

AN ODE TO EVERYONE
WHO HAS EVER
ROYALLY GOT ON YOUR NERVES.

You know exactly who you are,
But I won't put you to shame.
I kiss my mother with this mouth:
It will never speak your name.

Like an unrepentant sadist
You turn pain into an art.
Like galloping pneumonia
You penetrate my heart.

Like Frankenstein's assistant's
No-one likes your hunch.
Like the Tilt-A-Whirl at a funfair
You make me lose my lunch.

You put the bore in boardwalk
The lid on a holiday.
The moment you walk up to me
I want to walk away.

Every cat you ever owned
Took all of its nine lives.
You give me the home of a million bees
                                  Hives

Your median hateful quotient
Graphs on exponential curves.
Like an epic case of shingles
You get on all my nerves.

People lose the will to live
Whenever you come in
Murder's not an option—

You're not worth a mortal sin.

All of us have thought this
But not said it to your face:
Your sudden disappearance
Would improve the human race.

Everyone you drive past
Or who sees you on the road
Wishes that the car you're in
Would just up and explode.

When you walk it's like the summer—
We're waiting for the Fall.
Like a nice warm bowl of mayonnaise
You nauseate us all.

You got no style
You got no rhythm
Or idea what you get to do with 'em
You got no class
No social station
And precious little conversation

Whenever people smile at you
It's not some social game;
They're privately imagining you
Bursting into flame.

Everybody here
And that includes all of the staff
Eagerly awaits the day
They'll read your epitaph.

Like the Port-o-Sans at Woodstock
I think you're full of crap
I'm glad to state you're two-faced
'Cause that gives me more to slap.

Like a just-exploded pustule
You're splattered all about
Like a slob who doesn't exercise
You're just not working out

I think of Armageddon
Whenever you appear
In the sense that when you show up
Armageddon outta here!

You're invited to a picnic.
The other guest's a bear.
You're a lagomorph on the no-fly list
                              Unwanted hare.

Like a touch of poison ivy
You keep on blistering through.
Like an opera without music
You're not worth listening to.

I'd feed you to the zombies
But their staple food is brains,
So I'll feed you to piranhas
Set fire to the remains
Stamp on all your ashes
And flush them down the drain
Then build myself a time machine
And do it all again.

The parents that begat you
Violated nature's laws.
It would take a couple of terabytes
To catalogue your flaws.

We can't depend on magic,
Or Santa's helper elf,
So vis-a-vis your getting lost:
Take care that yourself.

THE CURSE ON MY FAMILY

On every family tree there is a blighted limb or two or three
And this applies especially to me
Five centuries ago my folk were not good folk
—in fact my family were reivers, one of thirty groups
that stole and threatened, burned and blackmailed,
stoked the anger of two nations we deceived.
We hopped the Scottish border into England, where we
Reived and reived and reived.

The Bishop of Glasgow knew our game
And wasn't happy that we did it
He loved the border and planned to rid it of our kind
before we escalated into crimes a level worse.
So he wrote a sermon, passed it round, to spread this deadly curse
on our sedition; his admonition
broadcast from the pulpit in this verse:

In the name of all that's holy, said he,
I curse the reivers, specifically…
I curse their heads their hair their eyes their teeth
Their hearts heads backs and bellies
And the bits that hang beneath
I curse them back and front from feet to tips of head
Their skin and all inside it —this I curse.

And the reivers reived on regardless
Unconcerned by how episcopally peeved this person was
So the bishop drew breath and inspiration
And continued with his curse this way:

I curse them when they go to ride
I curse them when they stay inside
I curse them sitting down to eat
I curse them lying down to sleep
Waking/walking, silent/talking, buying/selling, hunting/hawking
I curse their wives and children, friends and vendors and their kin
Anyone who aids them or profits from their crimes, I curse.

And the reivers went on reiving, leaving widows grieving
Not caring that some cleric was ranting and hysteric
So the bishop rolled up his sleeves,
inveighed against whoever reives
This conse crated vicar laid it on much thicker,
saying

I call a scourge upon their halls,
their cowsheds, kitchens, garden walls
Their cabbage patches, cows and sheep,
their plows, the chambers where they sleep
May all the woes from the books of Moses
light upon them–and their noses–
May floods and pestilence beset them,
and as for cures–may they never get them.
May their souls fall to the pit of hell,
and their hanging bodies never smell
Because each buzzard, dog and rat
shall eat them first. And that is that:
That's my curse, may it sit
upon all reivers, till they quit.

The Reivers reived some more,
but eventually they stopped.
My ancestors turned peasant.
They bred their own sheep, tilled the land,
and most of them were pleasant.

I've never reived myself,
so I'm not subject to this curse,
So mister bishop, sir, I'd like to ask of you:
About my hair and teeth and eyes
–is there something you can do?

AN IRISH HAIKU

CELEBRATING A BOSTONIAN
VIRGINIAN
NEW YORKER
PHILADELPHIAN
AND
POET
WHO LIVED AND DIED IN BALTIMORE
OR
I'M JUST A POE BOY
AND I DON'T MEAN AS IN THE SANDWICH

If it's good Gothic fun that you're cravin'
You don't have to start misbehavin'
A much better bet
Is the thrill that you get
From a good "Nevermore, quoth the Raven."